YOUR KNOWLEDGE HAS V

- We will publish your bachelor's and master's thesis, essays and papers

- Your own eBook and book - sold worldwide in all relevant shops

- Earn money with each sale

Upload your text at www.GRIN.com
and publish for free

Sven Weinzierl

Aus der Reihe: e-fellows.net stipendiaten-wissen

e-fellows.net (Hrsg.)

Band 1339

Big Data In-Memory Analytics explained by SAP HANA

GRIN Publishing

Bibliographic information published by the German National Library:

The German National Library lists this publication in the National Bibliography; detailed bibliographic data are available on the Internet at http://dnb.dnb.de .

Imprint:

Copyright © 2015 GRIN Verlag GmbH
Print and binding: Books on Demand GmbH, Norderstedt Germany
ISBN: 978-3-656-97081-1

This book at GRIN:

http://www.grin.com/en/e-book/300886/big-data-in-memory-analytics-explained-by-sap-hana

GRIN - Your knowledge has value

Since its foundation in 1998, GRIN has specialized In publishing academic texts by students, college teachers and other academics as e-book and printed book. The website www.grin.com is an ideal platform for presenting term papers, final papers, scientific essays, dissertations and specialist books.

Visit us on the internet:

http://www.grin.com/

http://www.facebook.com/grincom

http://www.twitter.com/grin_com

Big Data – In-memory analytics

by

Sven Weinzierl

Thesis Submitted in Partial Fulfillment

of the Requirements for the Degree of

Bachelor of Arts

Wirtschaftsinformatik

Hochschule Ansbach

15.04.2015

Abstract

Nowadays, people produce large amounts of data with talking via smartphones, reading e-mails or using platforms to find the appropriate partner. Conventional technologies no longer cope with the increasing amount of data and come to their limits. Therefore new technologies of Big Data are required for data processing to overcome the data flood.

At the beginning, this paper clarifies what Big Data is, the technologies of Big Data, how Big Data differs from Business Intelligence and a distinction is made between Data Warehouse and Business Intelligence. Furthermore, the theory of the Big Data technology in-memory analytics is explained and an implementation of this technology called "SAP HANA" is consulted and reviewed. In conclusion, the potential of in-memory analytics will be classified.

Table of contents

List of figures

1 Meaning of Big Data

Big Data is becoming increasingly important, not only in the world of information technology. The following graphic shows the application areas of Big Data.

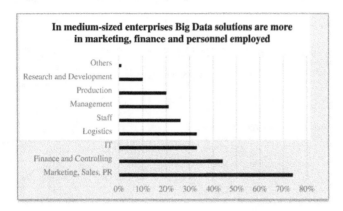

Figure 2-1: Use of Big Data in different application areas (BITKOM e.V., 2014)

Different interpretations and diverse reporting make it difficult to differ between hype and reality of Big Data. Therefore, the question arises – what Big Data exactly is? "Big Data […] describes large volumes of high velocity, complex and variable data that require advanced techniques and technologies to enable the capture, storage, distribution, management, and analysis of the information" (Agarwal, et al., 2012, pp. 9-15).

Further, characteristics of Big Data will be explained to make it possible to assess this technology. According to an article from the Harvard Business Review, Big Data is defined by the three dimensions volume, velocity and variety (McAfee & Brynjolfsson, 2012). Volume stands for data size. For in instance, it is estimated that Walmart collects more than two and a half petabytes of data every hour from its customers transactions – a petabyte is one quadrillion bytes, or the equivalent of about 20 million filing cabinets' worth of text (McAfee & Brynjolfsson, 2012). The second dimension is velocity and means the speed of data creation. With real-time or nearly real-time reporting the company can realize a competitive advantage, because the company is able to act more flexible than competition. Variety is the last dimension and covers the different data sources. In this context, data sources are affected, which stores structured, unstructured or semi-structured data. Michael Brands a specialist in analyzing of data says: "[…] it is generally acknowledged in modern economy that knowledge is the biggest of asset of companies and most of this knowledge, since it is developed by people, is recorded in unstructured formats" (Zicari, 2012). Therefore Big Data technologies are mainly focused on unstructured data.

2 Technologies of Big Data

To make it possible to efficiently process large amounts of data, new technologies are needed. The disciplines of Big Data are evolving so quickly that businesses need to wade in or risk being left behind (Mitchell, 2014). In the past, emerging technologies have taken years to mature. Now people iterate and drive solutions in a matter of months or even weeks. The following table faces the trends of Big Data. In chapter five the technology in-memory analytics will be explained in more detail.

Technology	Short description
Hadoop	Enterprise data operating system to perform many different data manipulations and analytics operations
Big data lakes / enterprise data hub	Organic data model for building large-scale databases
Predictive analytics	More historical data (a lot of records and attributes) to increase predictability
NoSQL	More efficient alternative of traditional relational based SQL
Deep learning	Enables computers to recognize items of interest in large quantities of unstructured and binary data and deduce relationships
In-memory analytics	Processing data in operative memory in-

	stead of hard drive memory

Table 1: Big Data technologies (Mitchell, 2014)

3 Big Data versus Business Intelligence

The market research company Gartner Inc. defines Business Intelligence as "[…] an umbrella term that includes the applications, infrastructure and tools, and best practices that enable access to and analysis of information to improve and optimize decisions and performance" (Gartner, Inc., 2015). The concepts of Business Intelligence and Big Data are often used in the same context. Therefore, these two concepts are now clearly distinguished from each other.

Eric Brown, a technology and marketing consultant, set apart Business Intelligence from Big Data by saying "Business Intelligence helps find answers to questions you know. Big Data helps you find the questions you don't know you want to ask" (Brown, 2014). That means Business Intelligence systems deliver clear answers for well-designed questions, based on persistent, structured and consistent data. By contrast within the scope of Big Data the companies do not know exactly what questions they need to be asking (Brown, 2014). According to a study of IDC over 90 percent of the digital universe consists of unstructured data (Gantz & Reinsel, 2011). Due to this, Big Data is mainly directed to unstructured data.

In order to make a clear distinction the three already mentioned dimensions for assessing Big Data are applied. The following figure makes an assignment of Big Data and Business Intelligence in relation to the dimensions volume and variety to clarify the difference of these two technical approaches. To reduce the complexity, the following figure does not include the third dimension velocity.

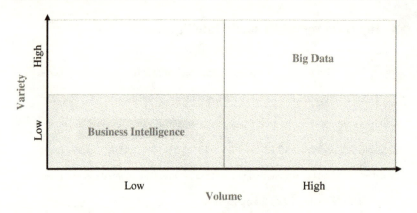

Figure 3-1: Classification of Big Data and Business Intelligence

4 Business Intelligence, Business Intelligence Framework

and Data Warehouse

Business Intelligence indicates an integrated, company-specific and it-specific global approach to support decision making (Kemper, Baars, & Mehanna, 2010, pp. 8-15). The configuration of this approach is made based on the Business Intelligence Framework that provides the space for a company-specific design. This framework is separated in the 3 layers, the data providing layer, the data analysis layer and the data presentation layer (Kemper, Baars, & Mehanna, 2010).

Furthermore, the term Data Warehouse is assigned the data providing layer. The father of Data Warehouse, William Inmon defines Data Warehouse as:" a subject-oriented, integrated, non-volatile and time-variant collection of data in support of management's decisions" (Inmon, 2005, p. 29). So Data Warehouse is the central component to collect data in context of the Business Intelligence approach.

5   In-memory analytics

Due to the increasing demands on systems for data analysis, a number of archi-

tectural approaches have emerged in recent years. The massive use of main memory is

one of these techniques, besides the use of special hardware or parallelization (Thiele,

Lehner, & Habich, 2011, pp. 57-67). Smaller main memories are used by Business In-

telligence systems for a long time (Funk, Marinkov, & Paar, 2012). However, to follow

these approaches, systems use huge RAM for data storage and management in connec-

tion with data analysis instead of hard disk drives. This enables a significantly shorten-

ing of response times. The following figure depicts a performance comparison of dif-

ferent database types.

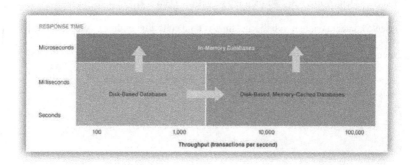

Figure 5-1: Performance comparision of different database types (Acker, Gröne,
       Blockus, & Bange, 2011, pp. 129-136)

By reducing the input-output-overhead, an optimization of read and write opera-

tions is achieved (Thiele, Lehner, & Habich, 2011, pp. 57-67). With respect to the

software, input-output-overhead is reduced by the column-oriented storage, the com-

pression of data, a two-stage buffer concept and the relocation of the computationally

intensive operations on database level (Thiele, Lehner, & Habich, 2011, pp. 57-67).

Regarding the hardware, a reduction of input-output-overhead is made by the extensive use of main memory, by which already smaller Data Warehouse scenarios are mapped

completely in main memory (Thiele, Lehner, & Habich, 2011, pp. 57-67). Therefore it

is clear that this combination of software and hardware approaches enables a higher

performance by reducing input-output-overhead. This means a shortening of the time

for processing analyses.

5.1   Example of implementation: SAP HANA

SAP HANA is a hybrid in-memory database. In the following, technical con-

cepts are explained which combines SAP HANA as an in-memory analytics implemen-

tation.

5.1.1   Technical concepts

Column-oriented storage

The difference between a column-oriented storage and a row-oriented storage

lies in the way as the data stored on the file system. Row-oriented storage means the

values of a row are stored sequentially. If the table contents are stored column-oriented,

data can be read without interruption and can be aggregated quickly, without jumping

from column to column as in a column-oriented database (Knötzele, 2013, pp. 381-

412). However, SAP HANA is a relational database whose tables can be stored in a

columnar format (Vezzosi, Le Bihan, Mazoué, & Imm, 2015, pp. 3-5).

Compression

If the tables are stored in a columnar format, SAP HANA enables a higher com-

pression-rate, because the values of a column have the same data type (Knötzele, 2013,

pp. 381-412). The use of compression allows a significant reduction of data volume and makes is possible to store huge databases complete in main memory (Thiele, Lehner, &

Habich, 2011, pp. 57-67). The reduction of data volume leads to a more effective use of

the valuable RAM. So the companies are able to decrease their costs for main memory.

Row- and column-oriented buffer

The usage of a column-oriented storage instead of a row-oriented storage leads

to a slowdown with respect to certain database operations. Especially the insert-

operations cause longer response times (Knötzele, 2013, pp. 381-412). To reduce the

response times and make the columns "write-optimized" SAP HANA applies a process

consisting of two buffers (Knötzele, 2013, pp. 381-412). First of all the new data record

will be written in a row-oriented buffer. After few seconds the data will be translated in

a column-oriented buffer and will be synchronized several times a day with the in-

memory database. The following figure illustrates the three phases of the mentioned

buffer concept.

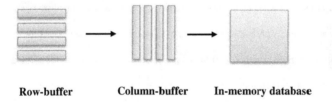

   Row-buffer   **Column-buffer**   **In-memory database**

Figure 5-2: Buffer concept of SAP HANA (Knötzele, 2013, pp. 381-412)

Transfer of computer intensive operations

The distribution of the application logic and database logic provides a bottle-

neck in today's systems (Knötzele, 2013, pp. 381-412). Generally SAP HANA enables

to run computationally and data intensive calculations directly in the database or close

to the persistence layer to avoid unnecessary transport of data in the application layer

(Seubert, 2013). Therefore logics are processed on the database server or SAP HANA database and only the results of the calculations will be transferred to the application layer.

5.1.2   SAP HANA and real-time

The term real-time is often directly used with SAP HANA. But what means real-time? In general, real-time is meant when the triggered operation has only a short delay, which does not influence the application itself or the human feeling (DATACOM Buchverlag GmbH, 2015). Beyond, the term real-time depends in this context on the size of main memory and the scope of analytics. According to IT-expert Ethan Jewett, the choice for SAP HANA depends on the management data needs. SAP Business Warehouse enables as well as real-time analytics but with respect to less extensive analyses (Jewett, 2012). Only the right combination of technology and the amount of data to be processed enables real-time processing. Therefore the terms real-time and SAP HANA are indirectly connected to each other.

5.1.3   Solutions of SAP HANA

There are two different solutions of SAP HANA. On the one hand SAP Business Warehouse powered by SAP HANA and on the other hand SAP HANA native. In November 2011, SAP released SAP Business Warehouse 7.3 powered by SAP HANA (SAP AG, 2014). With this release, the use of the SAP HANA in-memory database was possible on database layer next to the relational database management systems (Haun, Hickman, Loden, & Wells, 2013, pp. 36-39). The in-memory technique enables to solve speed problems of data providers in context of SAP Business Intelligence based on a relational database. SAP HANA native represents solutions that provision and access data within SAP HANA directly without any additional software layer like SAP

Business Intelligence. (Haun, Hickman, Loden, & Wells, 2013, pp. 40-43). So the per-

formance of such solutions will be unimpeded by additional software layers.

5.1.4 Review

The use of SAP HANA is context-dependent. In some scenarios a SAP Business

Warehouse powered by SAP HANA is completely sufficient. When the tuning possibil-

ities have been exhausted, SAP HANA native is an alternative for increasing data vol-

umes and more efficient data analysis which is not possible in traditional relational da-

tabase environments (Funk, Marinkov, & Paar, 2012). Furthermore, SAP HANA has

not a unique selling point because some competitors like Oracle offer similar solutions

(Opitz Consulting GmbH, 2014). Processing of the data in main memory is not a new

invention. The possibility to integrate SAP HANA in an implemented SAP landscape

and the fact that higher performance rates can be reached with an intelligent combina-

tion of software and hardware approaches make it very attractive for customers to

spend a lot of budget for it (Opitz Consulting GmbH, 2014).

5.2 Potential of in-memory analytics

According to Gartner's 2014 hype cycle for emerging technologies, the technol-

ogy in-memory analytics will reach the plateau of productivity in less than two years

(Rivera & Van der Meulen, 2014). In memory analytics has already overcome the hype

phase of expectations and gradually creates a tangible business value. Figure 4-3 repre-

sents Gartner's 2014 hype cycle.

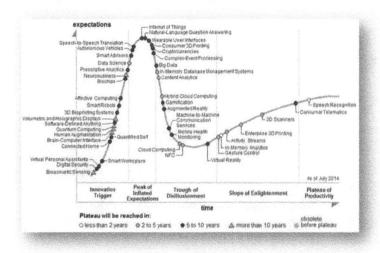

Figure 5-3: Hype cycle for emerging technologies (Rivera & Van der Meulen, 2014)
Zeier an in-memory data specialist from Accenture says: "in-memory processing repre-
sents the third era of computing [after the mainframe and client server computing era]"
(Zeier, 2014). This confirms the high potential of in-memory analytics.

References

Acker, O., Gröne, F., Blockus, A., & Bange, C. (2011). In-memory analytics –
strategies for real-time CRM. *Journal of Database Marketing & Customer
Strategy Management*, pp. 129-136.

Agarwal, M., Ajemian, S., Campbell, R., Coggeshall, S., Cull, B., Gillespie, E., & Igoe,
J. (2012). *Demystifying Big Data: A Practical Guide To Transforming The
Business of Government*. (T. F. Commission, Ed.) Retrieved April 01, 2015,
from http://www-
304.ibm.com/industries/publicsector/fileserve?contentid=239170

BITKOM e.V. (2014). *Potenziale und Einsatz von Big Data, Ergebnisse einer
repräsentativen Befragung von Unternehmen in Deutschland*. Retrieved April
02, 2015, from
http:www.bitkom.org/files/documents/Studienbericht_Big_Data_in_deutschen_
Unternehmen.pdf

Brown, E. (2014). *What's the difference between Business Intelligence and Big Data?*
Retrieved March 24, 2015, from http://ericbrown.com/whats-difference-
business-intelligence-big-data.htm

DATACOM Buchverlag GmbH. (2015). *Echtzeitanwendungen*. Retrieved March 30,
2015, from http://www.itwissen.info/definition/lexikon/Echtzeitanwendung-
realtime-application.html

Funk, M., Marinkov, B., & Paar, M. (2012). *Trends in der IT, In-Memory- Technologie*.
Retrieved April 04, 2015, from http://trends-in-der-it.de/?Fachartikel/In-
Memory-_Technologie

Gantz, J., & Reinsel, D. (2011). *Extracting Value from Chaos*. Retrieved March 26,
2015, from http://www.emc.com/collateral/analyst-reports/idc-extracting-value-
from-chaos-ar.pdf

Gartner, Inc. (2015). *Business Intelligence (BI)*. Retrieved March 26, 2015, from
http://www.gartner.com/it-glossary/business-intelligence-bi/

Haun, J., Hickman, C., Loden, D., & Wells, R. (2013). *Implementing SAP HANA* (1 ed.). Bosten: Galileo Press Inc.

Inmon, W. (2005). *Building the Data Warehouse* (4 ed.). Indianapolis: Wiley Publishing, Inc.

Jewett, E. (2012). *HANA or Business Warehouse? Choice depends on SAP data management needs.* Retrieved March 30, 2015, from http://searchsap.techtarget.com/feature/HANA-or-Business-Warehouse-Choice-depends-on-SAP-data-management-needs

Kemper, H.-G., Baars, H., & Mehanna, W. (2010). *Grundlagen und praktische Anwendungen, Eine Einführung in die IT-basierte Managementunterstützung* (3 ed.). Wiesbaden: Vieweg+Teubner Verlag.

Knötzele, T. (2013). SAP HANA. In L. Heilig, P. John, T. Kessler, T. Knötzele, & K. Thaler-Mieslinger, *SAP NetWeaver BW und SAP Business Objects - Das umfassende Handbuch* (2 ed., pp. 381-412). Bonn: Galileo Press.

McAfee, A., & Brynjolfsson, E. (2012). *Big Data: The Management Revolution.* Retrieved March 26, 2015, from https://hbr.org/2012/10/big-data-the-management-revolution

Mitchell, R. (2014). *Big data technologies and practices are moving quickly. Here's what you need to know to stay ahead of the game.* Retrieved March 24, 2015, from http://www.computerworld.com/article/2690856/8-big-trends-in-big-data-analytics.html

Opitz Consulting GmbH. (2014). *SAP HANA versus Oracle, In-Memory-Systeme im Vergleich.* Retrieved from http://www.opitz-consulting.com/fileadmin/redaktion/veroeffentlichungen/whitepaper/whitepaper-sap-hana-versus-oracle_sicher.pdf

Rivera, J., & Van der Meulen, R. (2014). *Gartner's 2014 Hype Cycle for Emerging Technologies Maps the Journey to Digital Business.* Retrieved March 31, 2015, from http://www.gartner.com/newsroom/id/2819918

SAP AG. (2014). *SAP Business Warehouse 7.3*. Retrieved April 14, 2015, from scn.sap.com/docs/DOC-8683

Seubert, H. (2013). *SAP HANA als Entwicklungsplattform, Mehr als eine Datenbank*. Retrieved March 25, 2015, from https://entwickler.de/online/datenbanken/mehr-als-eine-datenbank-115887.html

Thiele, M., Lehner, W., & Habich, D. (2011). Innovative Unternehmensanwendungen mit In-Memory Data Management, Beiträge der Tagung IMDM 2011. *Data-Warehousing 3.0 – Die Rolle von Data-Warehouse Systemen auf Basis von In-Memory-Technologie* (pp. 57-68). Mainz: Köllen Druck+Verlag GmbH.

Turner, V., Reinsel, D., Gantz, J., & Minton, S. (2014). *The Digital Universe of Opportunities: Rich Data and the Increasing Value of the Internet of Things*. Retrieved March 24, 2015, from http://idcdocserv.com/1678

Vezzosi, P., Le Bihan, P., Mazoué, D., & Imm, E. (2015). Creating a universe on SAP HANA. pp. 3-5.

Zeier, A. (2014). Interview: Accenture's in-memory data guru, Alexander Zeier. (C. Saran, Interviewer) Retrieved March 26, 2015, from http://www.computerweekly.com/news/2240171238/Interview-Accentures-in-memory-data-guru-Alexander-Zeier

Zicari, R. (2012). *On Analyzing Unstructured Data. — Interview with Michael Brands*. Retrieved April 02, 2015, from http://www.odbms.org/blog/2012/07/on-analyzing-unstructured-data-interview-with-michael-brands/